# WHAT DO THE ANIMALS SAY?

## IN THE WINTER

By H. A. Schubert

Dear Friends,

Children often love animals of all sorts! In this book, *What Do the Animals Say?* you will have the unique and fun opportunity to share stories about what the animals photographed in the winter might be saying. This book comes even more alive when you encourage a child's use of their imagination to describe what he or she thinks the animals are saying! You can use the lined space provided to document your young charges thoughtful, creative and sometimes quite humorous ideas! *What Do the Animals Say?* is sure to be a book to return to again & again as a childhood favorite and as a lovely recorder of shared memories!

Do you think there are animals in these woods?
What do you think they are doing?...
Let's look at some animals in the winter and
explore what they might be saying!

Ahhh, I feel *so* much better sitting in the snow!! -I'm so hot in all of this fur!

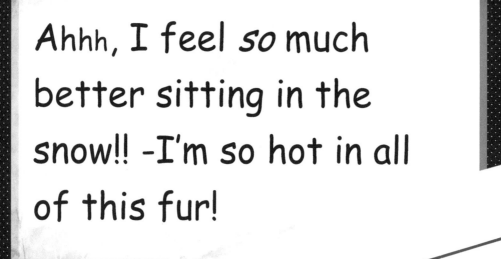

Bear (unidentified)

Oh boy, somebody filled our favorite feeder! ... it's dinner-time!!

_____

_____

_____

_____

_____

Birds (unidentified)

White Swans

Polar bear

White horse

Weddell Seal pup

My parents say owls are wise... so why am I sitting in the snow, talking with my eyes closed?! -Silly me!

Snowy Owl

YUM! I love finding my favorite berries in the winter!!

Waxwing

Hide and Seek is fun!
- I wonder where my
friends are hiding?!

_____

_____

_____

_____

_____

Red Fox

Family picture time! Let's all look at the camera please!

Emperor Penguins

Lynx

OOPS! I slipped and slid to the edge of the ice! ...what do you think I should do?

Common Seal

Grizzly Bear

Basset Hound

My favorite thing to do in the winter is to run around and around!!

Brown Horse

Young striped cat

Yum! There's nothing like being in a nice little house having my favorite snack!!

Squirrel

We hope you have enjoyed this book!

Here is an additional title from H.A. Schubert you may like:

Additional interesting titles can be found on Heights Publishing's website:
Https://HeightsPublishing.com or you can find us by searching for Heights Publishing on Amazon or Barnes and Noble.

Heights Publishing
Cleveland, Ohio

The author acknowledges with appreciation the following artists (featured in Adobe Stock) whose work is found in this book:

Book cover art: copyright ©2017 © Jamrooferpix © james_pintar © ksuksa

Book interior:
Photographic art: copyright © 2017 © Krzysztof Wiktor ©Byrdyak © Vera Kuttelvaserova © Shaiith ©Vladimir Melnik © terex © pilipenkod © james_pintar ©Maslov Dmitry © seread © Silver © Kyslynskyy © ijdema © seread © ksuksa © Melory © Patryssia © bubblegirlphoto

Textbox background art: copyright © 2017 © bluesky © orangeberry © anilin © Liliia © Liliia © oly5 © songglod © undrey © Ivana Rauski © Terriana © Jamrooferpix © Jamrooferpix © songglod © flowerstock © kaidash © flas100

*Please note that all animal identification placed under each respective photograph is per the photographer's notation.

CPSIA information can be obtained
at www.ICGtesting.com
Printed in the USA
BVHW021655031220
594827BV00036B/52